ABC Acadie

ABC

"Mémère, please tell us again about when you were little. Tell us about the Acadians."

"That was oh so long ago when I was young like you. And oh so far away from the Louisiana bayou where we live now. And yet, when I remember, it seems like only yesterday. But gather round grandchildren — Pélagie, Sophie, and Nicolas — so you can hear me tell the story as your Uncle Samuel plays his fiddle softly on the gallery."

ABC Acadie

Mary Alice Downie

Illustrated by
Anne LeBlanc

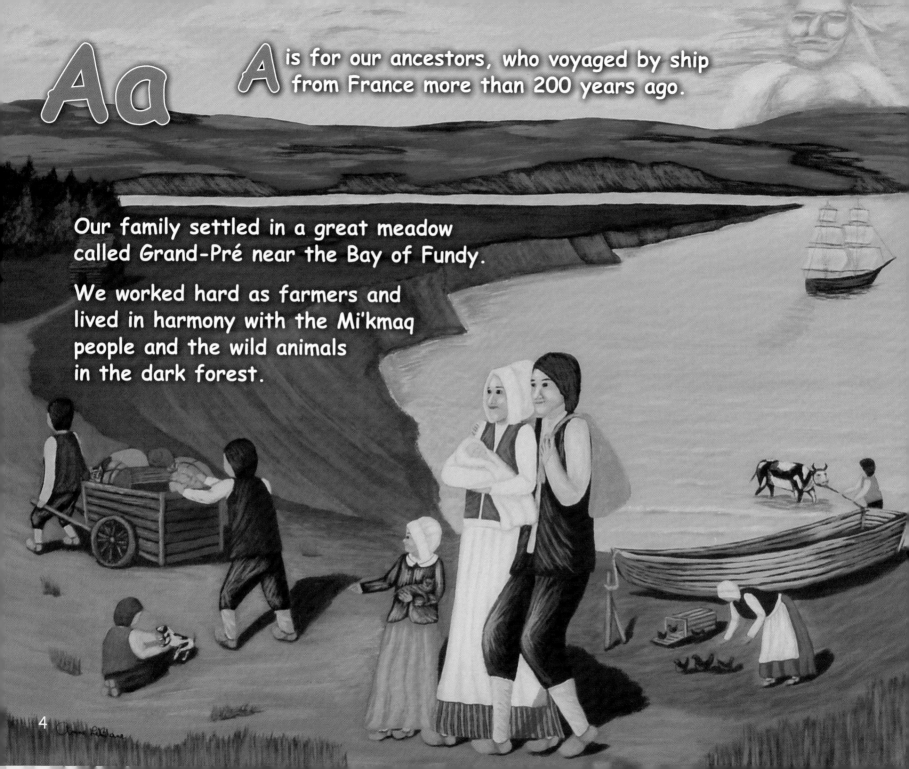

Aa **A** is for our ancestors, who voyaged by ship from France more than 200 years ago.

Our family settled in a great meadow called Grand-Pré near the Bay of Fundy.

We worked hard as farmers and lived in harmony with the Mi'kmaq people and the wild animals in the dark forest.

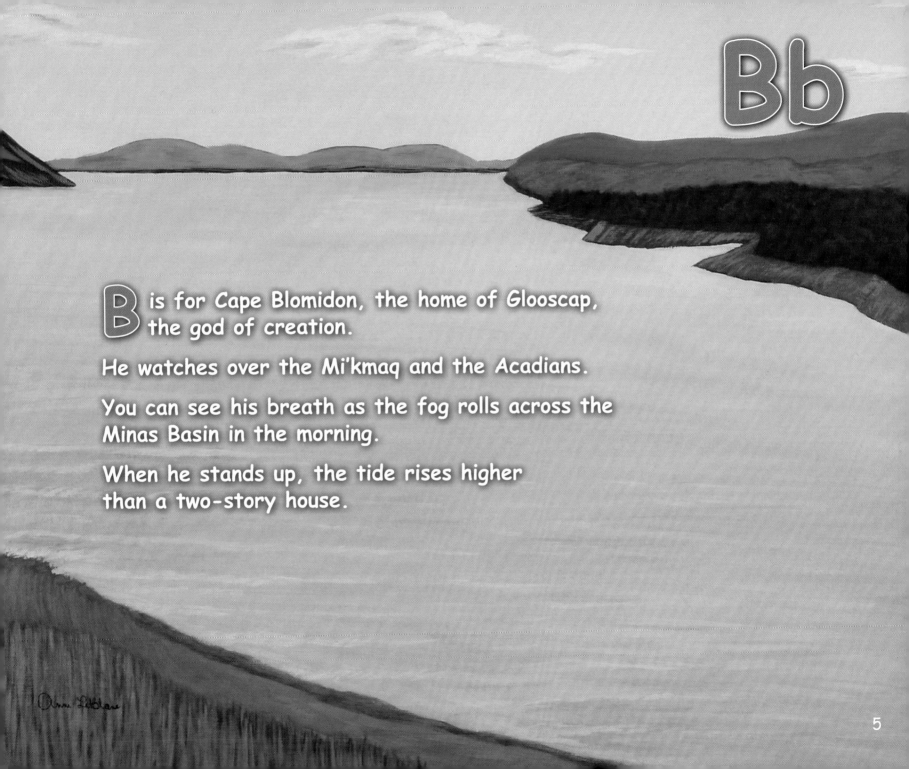

B is for Cape Blomidon, the home of Glooscap, the god of creation.

He watches over the Mi'kmaq and the Acadians.

You can see his breath as the fog rolls across the Minas Basin in the morning.

When he stands up, the tide rises higher than a two-story house.

C is for my cousin Clément. He is a blacksmith. After dinner he tells us magical stories.

"Beware of goblins at night," he told us. "Werewolves, will o' the wisps — and the Devil's white horse!"

To ward off these scary beasts, he made me a horseshoe from a piece of iron left over after shoeing an ox.

D is for dikes, built to flood and drain the salt water from the marshes. As the years passed, the land became rich enough to grow our crops of wheat, rye, oats, and peas to make soup.

Ee

E is for the eagle, king of the birds. From their huge nests at the top of the trees they reigned over the fox, lynx, wolf, and the bear on the forest floor.

Whenever I see an eagle soaring overhead,
my spirits are lifted and I dream
that one day we might
return to our home
in Acadie.

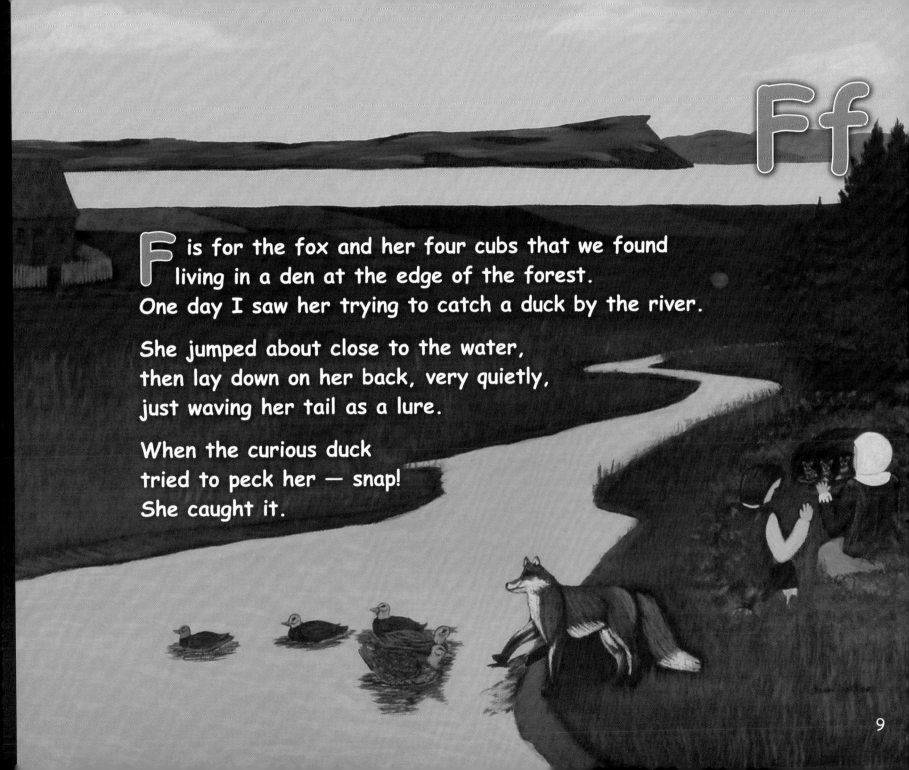

F is for the fox and her four cubs that we found
living in a den at the edge of the forest.
One day I saw her trying to catch a duck by the river.

She jumped about close to the water,
then lay down on her back, very quietly,
just waving her tail as a lure.

When the curious duck
tried to peck her — snap!
She caught it.

9

Gg

G is for the games we played when we finished our chores for the day. Button, Button, or Blind Man's Buff, or Puss-In-The-Corner. My brother Gaston would pretend to be a ghost and we would all run and hide.

H is for the harvest festival held every year. The apples and vegetables were stored in big baskets in the stone-walled cellars beneath the houses. The whole village gathered in the churchyard to give thanks for the bounty of the land.

Hh

11

Ii

I is for the ice that covered the ocean flats and riverbanks. It floated up and down with the changing of the tide. At low tide we climbed under the ice to dig for clams and crabs. "Stay back from the edge!" Nicolas warned, "You might slide into the freezing water!"

J is for the noisy Jaybird — and my little brother Jacques, who was even noisier. My mother told us she had found him under a cabbage in the garden. When he got into trouble, we all joined in to shout, "Take him back!"

K **k**

K is for my kitten Grisette. She was an ancestor of your cat, who sailed with us as a stowaway when we were expelled from Acadie.

Grisette always played with my knitting and turned it into a tangle of knots.
  "Nicolas, don't look so sad. Your dog is an Acadian too — and a scallywag!"

14

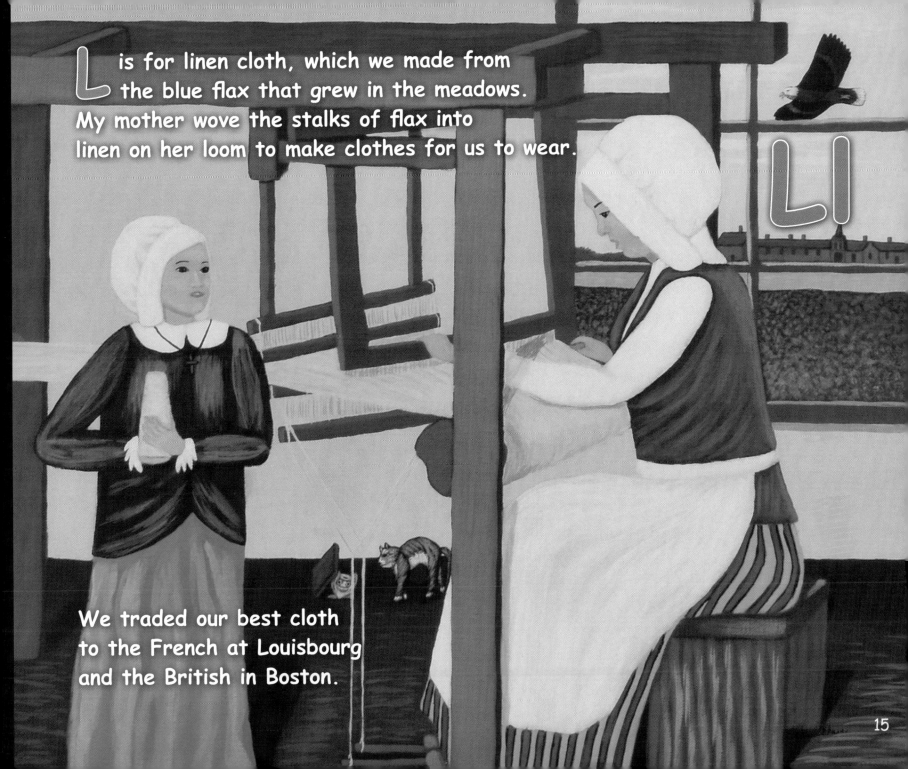

L is for linen cloth, which we made from
  the blue flax that grew in the meadows.
My mother wove the stalks of flax into
linen on her loom to make clothes for us to wear.

Ll

We traded our best cloth
to the French at Louisbourg
and the British in Boston.

15

Mm

M is for the Mi'kmaq, who were living in Acadie long before we arrived. They brought us furs and soft moccasins made of moose skin. I had a special pair with beads and ribbons.

N is for New Year's Day, when we celebrated throughout the village. My father and brothers went from house to house. They hugged everyone and asked forgiveness for things said and done.

Nn

O *o*

O is for our orchards, where apple, pear, plum, and cherry trees grew in rows. We planted willows to protect the fruit trees from the winter frost and wind.

18

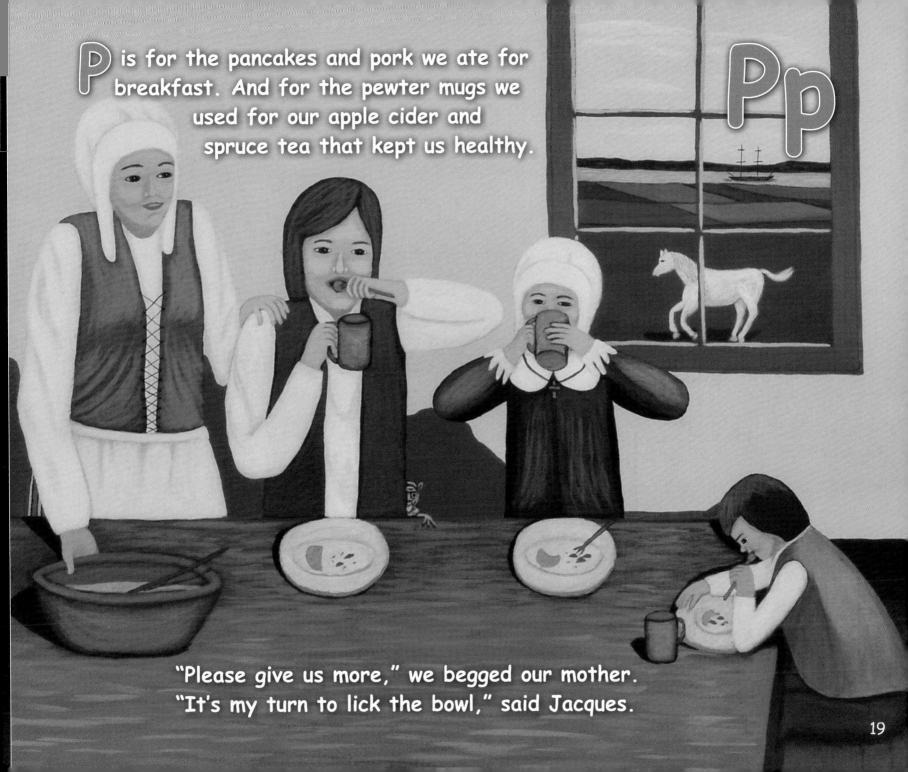

P is for the pancakes and pork we ate for breakfast. And for the pewter mugs we used for our apple cider and spruce tea that kept us healthy.

Pp

"Please give us more," we begged our mother.
"It's my turn to lick the bowl," said Jacques.

19

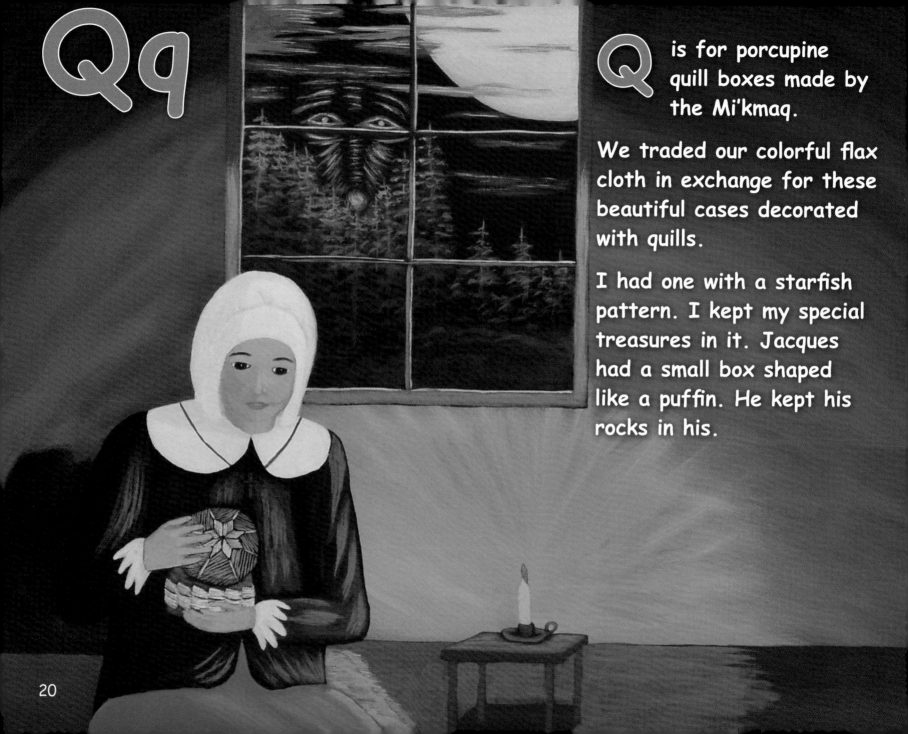

Qq

Q is for porcupine quill boxes made by the Mi'kmaq.

We traded our colorful flax cloth in exchange for these beautiful cases decorated with quills.

I had one with a starfish pattern. I kept my special treasures in it. Jacques had a small box shaped like a puffin. He kept his rocks in his.

Rr

R is for my rag doll. I left her out in the rain. I thought she was ruined. My sister Mathilde repaired her, as good as new, and decorated her with a red ribbon. "Sister, thank you for mending my doll," I told her. "I really like the ribbon!"

21

Ss

S is for snowshoes, which we wore to travel through the woods in the winter. Otherwise, we would have sunk up to our middles in snow. Of course, we don't need snowshoes in the bayou. We get around in boats but need to keep our eyes open for alligators and snakes.

T is for turnips, so tender and sweet. We roasted them in the fireplace ashes like chestnuts. On special days, my mother made our favorite turnip-cabbage soup.

"Here you go my children. You've been so good!"

23

Uu

U is for my great uncle Ulysse, who was a ship's captain. He sailed back and forth from France to Acadie. One time he brought us all umbrellas in every color under the sun.

24

Oh — we had so much fun that day, but oh how things soon changed. Our family was scattered to the winds, like the umbrellas.

V is for the terrible voyage we were forced to take during the war between England and France.

The British soldiers burnt our houses, separated our families, and herded us onto the boats as if we were cattle. They didn't trust us because we spoke French.

W is for willow whistles, which we blew to alert everyone to danger. Some of our neighbors hid from the British in the forest, but most of our village was forced to leave until the war was over. Never to return.

X is for Exile. Our families were broken up and taken to faraway places. We had little to comfort us but our memories, until at last we came to Louisiana. We are happy enough in our new world, but we still remember our old ways.

Y is for the yawl, a small boat that brought us ashore on this bayou. We have lived ever since in our house on stilts, among the oaks, the Spanish moss, the ibis — and the alligators!

Yy

29

Zz

Z is the sound we make
as we fall asleep listening
to your Uncle play his fiddle.
It is so soothing. ZZZZZ

"Mémère, Mémère!
Wake up. Wake up!
I want to tell you what I'm
going to do when I grow up."

"What is that, Pélagie?"
"I'm going home to Acadie!"

31

Sources

ABC Acadie is a portrait of family life in Acadia a few years before the Grand Dérangement (1755) destroyed a gentle and pastoral society. This story is chiefly based on accounts by such early French explorers and travelers as the surgeon and botanist Le Sieur de Dièreville (1699-1711), who spent a year in the new colony, and Nicolas Denys (1598-1698), who settled permanently and wrote what is regarded as the best description of the customs of the Souriquois native people, now called the Mi'kmaq.

Cajuns [page 2-3]

Many Acadians were shipped to the 13 American Colonies, where they were often turned away or treated almost as slaves. Some were expelled to France, England, and the West Indies. Approximately 1500 were sent to the more welcoming Roman Catholic Spanish colony of Louisiana. The majority came later between 1765 and 1785. They adapted happily to a very different life in the bayous. It was warm! They created a new society and became known as the Cajuns. They retain strong ties with their northern cousins and many return every five years for Le Congrès Mondial Acadian.

First Settlement [page 4-5]

The Mi'kmaq were the first settlers of what became known as Acadie. On June 26, 1604, the French explorers Le Sieur de Monts and Samuel de Champlain attempted a settlement on an island in the Ste-Croix River. After a disastrous winter — half the crew died of scurvy — they tried again. In June 1605, they established the Habitation at Port-Royal, this time successfully, with the famous Order of Good Cheer to brighten the winter. The major population arrived in 1636 when several families arrived from Poitou, Normandy, and Brittany. There were a few hundred Acadians in the first census in 1671 who had settled in Grand-Pré on the Minas Basin, and more than 13,000 by 1755.

Blacksmith [page 6]

Lame Hephaestus was the Greek god of fire, metalworking, and sculpture. The Romans called him Vulcan. From ancient times the blacksmith has been a central figure in every community, forging horseshoes, tools, and utensils of iron. The hero's father in Henry Wadsworth Longfellow's famous Acadian poem, Évangéline, is a blacksmith:

Swiftly they hurried away to the forge of Basil the blacksmith.
There at the door they stood, with wondering eyes to behold him
Take in his leathern lap the hoof of the horse as a plaything,
Nailing the shoe in its place; while near him the tire of the cart-wheel
Lay like a fiery snake, coiled round in a circle of cinders.

The Acadians loved telling stories and making up legends. The white horse was the symbol of a man who sold his soul to the devil and

was possessed by him. It was said that this person could transform his body into a white horse. Another frightening being possessed by the devil was the werewolf, who transformed himself into a wolf or large dog at night and terrified everyone. Les feux follets or will o' the wisps were thought to be evil spirits rising up from the marsh or cemetery. In those days, anything that seemed suspicious was blamed on the devil. Goblins supposedly came on ships with the explorers. Although no one has ever seen them, these mischievous creatures made the horses run all night so that they were too tired to work the next morning. They also fed the horses too much, which made them fat.

Dikes [page 7]

The British thought that the Acadian colonists were lazy because instead of attempting the backbreaking work of clearing the forest, they used a technique remembered from their ancestors in France. Everyone worked together to build earthen dikes in the marshlands. In the base was a hinged wooden valve (*aboiteau*) with swinging doors. At low tide, the gate opened to let the fresh water out; at high tide, the gate was pushed shut, which kept out the salt water. After a few years they had rich fields for their crops. For fishing, they had another labor-saving method. They installed wooden stakes in a circle at low tide at the mouth of streams and rivers. When the tide came in, the fish were trapped inside the circle. When the tide went out, the fishermen simply walked over and gathered their catch.

Eagle and Fox [page 8-9]

The Eagle, Overlord of all the Birds,
Is common in these climes, and in the Woods
Builds his enormous nest; he who knows where,
And to it turns his steps, will find about
The tree, fragments enough to feed at least
Two families.

Dièreville described all sorts of birds, many not to be seen in France. He was particularly fond of the hummingbird, which he called, "The prettiest creatures in the world, whose coloring is so vivid, especially on the breast of the male, that in certain positions it seems to flash fire."

The neighboring forest was home to lynx, bears, fox, and wolves. Nicolas Denys says, "As for the Lynxes, if the Indians meet them and they or their Dogs pursue them, this animal mounts into a tree where it is easily killed, whilst the Dogs are terrifying it with their barkings. All the other animals are not really difficult to kill, and there is not one of them capable of attacking a man, at least unless it be attacked first. They kill with the arrow only all kinds of game, both water and land, whether flying or upon the ground. As for the Squirrel, the Partridge, and other small game, it is the children who amuse themselves with that."

Nicolas Denys also describes how dogs were trained to use the same hunting techniques. The hunter on the shore would hide, leaving the dog to run up and down. The hunter would toss a stick in the air and the birds would come closer to watch. And then the hunter would shoot.

Games [page 10]

Everyone helped with the chores, like bringing in wood and water, or helping with the dishes, but there was still time for play with games like Bouton (Button, Button); Colin-Maillard (Blind Man's Buff); Quatre-Coins (Puss-In-The-Corner.) In winter there was tobogganing and sledding, and ball in summer. The Mi'kmaq played a dice game called Waites, which still exists today, and a stick-and-ball game, which some think was an early form of hockey.

Harvest Festival [page 11]

In the midst of their hard work, the Acadians celebrated many festivals, including the Festival of the Geese when the birds returned in spring. Everyone gathered in the churchyard for prayers.

Icicles [page 12]

Apart from the normal tasks of caring for their flocks of sheep, in winter the men cut timber for fuel and fences, repaired tools for spring, and built new furniture. The women made clothing, blankets, and rag rugs. Most nights there were parties — they seem to have been a gregarious bunch — where they talked, sang, and put on plays. Le Théâtre de Neptune, by Marc Lescarbot (c. 1570-1642), was the first play recorded in North America by Europeans. It was performed in barges and canoes at Port-Royal on November 14, 1606 in honor of Samuel de Champlain and Jean de Biencourt de Poutrincourt, who were returning from exploring the coast as far south as Cape Cod. A court of Tritons and Aboriginals recited verse in French, Gascon, and Souriquois to an accompaniment of trumpets and cannons.

Jaybird [page 13]

According to the *Encyclopedia of Acadian Life*, "When it was time for the birth to occur, other children in the family were sent to stay with relatives. When the children returned to find a new baby, they would be told that the baby had been found under a cabbage, in the hay, a pond, or somewhere else nearby. Sometimes they told them that someone had brought the baby to them. Some other excuse was given to explain why the mother, who normally worked all day, needed to stay in bed."

Kitten [page 14]

Cats were brought on ships from France to help control the mice. They might be named after their color — Noireau, Blanchette, or Grisette — Malin if they had a bad temper, Mitaine if their paws were different. The Acadians had many animals. They kept sheep, cattle, goats, and chickens, oxen for ploughing, and small strong horses for riding and carrying loads. Pigs ranged freely in the woods.

Linen [page 15]

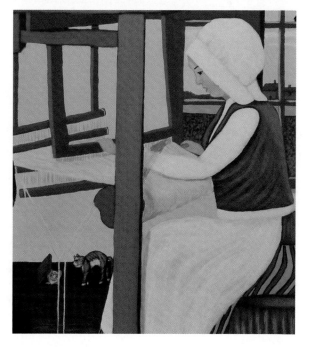

Flax was spun into thread to make linen for summer clothes. In winter they wore wool from their sheep and furs from hunting bears, beavers, foxes, otter, and martens. Preparing clothes was so much work that they kept them for a long time. One observer wrote, "The women's clothes are good enough, but they look as if they were pitched on with pitchforks." Andrew Brown said, "They had only two dyes, green and a grey black; both obtained from vegetable substances, & equally divided between the population; the green being appropriated to the young, and the grey black to the old," but another commented, "They were fond of black and red with stripes down the leg, bunches of ribbon and long streamers," which sounds jollier.

Mi'kmaq [page 16]

Once again, Denys has left us a vivid description: "They also make moccasins of their old robes of Moose skin, which are greasy and better than new. Their moccasins are rounded in front, and the sewing redoubles on the end of the foot, and is puckered as finely as a chemise. It is done very neatly; the girls make them for themselves embellished with colors, the seams being ornamented with quills of Porcupine, which they dye red and violet." Superb craftsmen, they made jewelry from shells and animal teeth and claws. Purple and blue 'beads' from mollusks were a particular favorite. Later they used glass beads and ribbons that were introduced by the Europeans. Lucky babies were wrapped in the softest skins of foxes, swans, and wild geese.

New Year's Day [page 17]

This festival was considerably more important than Christmas, which was a religious holiday celebrated with Midnight Mass and a crèche. The only gift was a Nolet, a kind of gingerbread. In the morning on New Year's Day, the men and boys visited each house in the village and embraced everyone there. The first person to enter had to be a young man. It was believed that a girl brought ill fortune to the family — like the Scottish tradition at Hogmanay, when a dark-haired young man must enter first. Then everyone went to the burial ground to remember lost relatives.

Orchard [page 18]

Apple trees were planted in close rows, protected by a wide belt of willows from the frosts of spring and the winds of autumn. They also had pears, cherry, and plum trees. There was a small arbor decorated with wild flowers, a floral playpen for children. Sunday nights they held services there. It was also a favorite spot for flirting.

Pancakes [page 19]

They ate locally and seasonally, breakfasting early on pancakes mixed with slices of fried pork, with water and milk to drink. Dinner might be beef or mutton, although Dièreville said, "Their favorite meat is that of the pig." Supper was a light meal of different kinds of milk and cream.

Quill boxes [page 20]

The Mi'kmaq were so skilled with quillwork that the French sometimes called them the Porcupine People. Lescarbot wrote, "They make.... works worthy of admiration, with the hairs [quills] colored with red, black, white and blue…so lively that ours seem in nothing to be comparable to them." These objects, like their elegant woven baskets, were much prized by Europeans.In later times, they even made mosaics of their brightly-colored quillwork birchbark on panels for chairs and tables.You can see samples in the Nova Scotia Museum of Natural History in Halifax.

Rag doll [page 21]

Toys were homemade, of course.

Snowshoes [page 22]

These were another Mi'kmaq invention. They had different sorts for different weather. Other useful inventions were canoes and toboggans.

Turnips [page 23]

Marc Lescarbot described planting the first European garden at Port-Royal: "The pleasure which I took in digging and tilling my gardens, fencing them in against the gluttony of the swine, making terraces, preparing straight alleys, building store-houses, sowing wheat, rye, barley, oats, beans, peas, garden plants, and watering them, so great a desire had I to know the soil by personal experience." The Acadians grew many vegetables: carrots, beets, turnips, onions and squashes of all sorts of shapes and colors, as well as parsnips and herbs. In the fall, the women stored them in big baskets in the stone-walled cellars beneath the houses. They pulled the cabbages, but left them in the fields, with their stalks sticking up, to be covered by snow and brought in later when needed. They ate only the hearts and fed the rest to the pigs. The woods were filled with blackberries, raspberries, and strawberries. And let's not forget maple syrup. Although it was a healthy diet, they avoided mushrooms. Dièreville wrote, "As a most potent Poison, they [the Acadians] regard/The Mushroom; nor by eating it would they/Make widows of their wives."

Umbrellas [page 24-25]

Umbrellas (ombrella: "little shadow") have been around for 4,000 years in Egypt, Greece, Assyria, and China. They were used as parasols to shade the lofty from the sun. The Chinese were the first to wax and laquer them as protection from the rain. Common in France from around 1620, they were not popular until the eighteenth century in England.

Voyage [page 26]

During the Grand Dérangement, many of the overcrowded ships sank and the people drowned. By 1764, they were allowed to return, but the fertile land had been granted to New England "Planters," so the Acadians were settled on the rocky shores of Nova Scotia and New Brunswick.

Willows [page 27]

These trees were very important. You can always tell where an Acadian house once stood if there are willows nearby. (In Eastern Ontario, if there are lilacs, there would have been a farmhouse.) Grand-Pré was totally destroyed apart from the dikelands and a row of ancient willows during the Expulsion. In 2012, "The Landscape of Grand-Pré" was listed as a UNESCO World Heritage site.

Expulsion [page 28]

1755 is the infamous date when British troops fell upon the Acadians, although removals continued for several years. Buildings were burned, crops and animals confiscated. Families were often separated as the people were herded onto ships in miserable conditions with only the clothes on their backs and the few possessions they could carry. Some hid in the woods or escaped to Quebec.

Yawl [page 29]

A yawl is a ship's small boat used to row passengers to shore when the water is shallow.

Zzz [page 30-31]

The Acadians brought their songs and hymns with them to Louisiana, and perhaps a few fiddles. It was tempting to use zydeco for z, but this popular form of music, a mix of Creole, Afro-American, and Cajun, came much later, after they had been long settled in the bayou. Sometimes known as swamp pop, instruments included accordions, guitars, drums, and fiddles and spoons. *Acadian Driftwood: The Roots of Acadian and Cajun Music* traces the rich history of music among these people.

Copyright and dedication

"They are now being reborn in Louisiana, and if they are helped a little, they will accomplish wonders."
– Aubry to Choiseul-Stainville. New Orleans, May 14, 1765

MAD *For Jack, who counts …*

AL *To all my Acadian ancestors who persevered through unthinkable hardship, thus allowing me to be the person I am, a French-speaking Acadian.*

Text © Mary Alice Downie, 2014.

Ilustrations © Anne LeBlanc, 2014.

All rights reserved.

Catalog in publication information available from the Library and Archives Canada and the Library of Congress.

ISBN 978-1-55082-383-7

Edited by Bob Hilderley.

Designed by Susan Hannah.

Printed and bound in Canada.

Published by Quarry Heritage Books, an imprint of Quarry Press, Inc.

PO Box 1061, Kingston, Ontario K7M 4Y5 www.quarrypress.com

FSC
MIX
Paper from responsible sources
www.fsc.org FSC® C107923